ALLIGATOR OR CROCODILE?

By Rob Ryndak

Gareth Stevens
PUBLISHING

Please visit our website, www.garethstevens.com. For a free color catalog of all our high-quality books, call toll free 1-800-542-2595 or fax 1-877-542-2596.

Library of Congress Cataloging-in-Publication Data

Ryndak, Rob, author.
 Alligator or crocodile? / Rob Ryndak.
     pages cm. — (Animal look-alikes)
 Includes bibliographical references and index.
 ISBN 978-1-4824-2708-0 (pbk.)
 ISBN 978-1-4824-2709-7 (6 pack)
 ISBN 978-1-4824-2710-3 (library binding)
 1. Alligators—Juvenile literature. 2. Crocodiles—Juvenile literature. I. Title.
 QL666.C925R96 2016
 0 597.98—dc23
                                        2014048824

Published in 2016 by
Gareth Stevens Publishing
111 East 14th Street, Suite 349
New York, NY 10003

Designer: Sarah Liddell
Editor: Ryan Nagelhout

Photo credits: Cover, p. 1 (background) Virunja/Shutterstock.com; cover, p. 1 (alligator) chloe7992/Shutterstock.com; cover, p. 1 (crocodile) seaskylab/Shutterstock.com; pp. 5, 21 Filipe Frazao/Shutterstock.com; p. 7 (caiman) sisqopote/Shutterstock.com; p. 7 (alligator) Songquan Deng/Shutterstock.com; p. 7 (crocodile) Naypong/Shutterstock.com; p. 9 Orhan Cam/Shutterstock.com; p. 11 Alex_Crimea/Shutterstock.com; p. 13 (alligator) Raffaella Calzoni/Shutterstock.com; p. 13 (crocodile) HaufFoto/Shutterstock.com; p. 15 (main) Samantzis/Shutterstock.com; p. 15 (inset) Curioso/Shutterstock.com; p. 17 kiwibritkaren/Shutterstock.com; p. 18 Gerrit_de_Vries/Shutterstock.com; p. 19 (alligator) Juan Gracia/Shutterstock.com; p. 19 (crocodile) defpicture/Shutterstock.com.

Printed in the United States of America

CPSIA compliance information: Batch #CS15GS: For further information contact Gareth Stevens, New York, New York at 1-800-542-2595.

CONTENTS

Boldface words appear in the glossary.

Hiding Below

The river looks calm, but what's that poking out of the water? Are those the eyes of an alligator, or is a crocodile ready to jump out and bite its dinner? Though they look very much alike, there are big differences between alligators and crocodiles.

Alligators and crocodiles share many features. They're both **reptiles** that have sharp teeth and spend lots of time in the water. Alligators and crocodiles—as well as animals called caimans—belong to a group of animals called Crocodilia.

CAIMAN

ALLIGATOR

CROCODILE

7

U or V?

Alligators and crocodiles have different-shaped heads. This means alligators and crocodiles each have a different bite! An alligator has a short, wide, U-shaped **snout**. This gives gators a strong bite used to **crush** turtle shells and other animals it eats.

ALLIGATOR

9

A crocodile has a narrower snout than an alligator. The teeth on each side of its mouth are closer together, which creates a longer, V-shaped head. Crocodiles eat all kinds of animals, and their jaws help them snag their meals.

CROCODILE

Gator and croc teeth are different, too. Alligators have a wide upper jaw that hides most of their lower teeth. Crocodiles commonly show more teeth, especially their bottom teeth. The fourth tooth on the bottom part of a crocodile's jaw can be seen when its mouth is closed.

ALLIGATOR

FOURTH TOOTH

CROCODILE

13

Salty Crocs

Crocodiles can be found all over the world, most often in salt water. They have special body parts on their tongue called glands that help them get rid of salt in their body. This lets them live in salt water longer than other members of the Crocodilia group.

SALT GLANDS

Alligators only live in China and the southeastern part of the United States. They usually live in freshwater **swamps**, lakes, and rivers. Alligators also have glands to help get rid of salt, but scientists think they don't work as well as the glands in crocodiles.

Special Sensors

Crocs and alligators have small sensors in pits on their body. These small dots help them sense **pressure** changes in water and find **prey**. Crocodiles have these spots all over their body, but alligators only have them around their jaws.

CROCODILE SENSOR

ALLIGATOR

CROCODILE

HOW CAN YOU TELL?

ANIMAL	ALLIGATOR	CROCODILE
LOCATION	United States, China	all over the world
WATER TYPE	mostly freshwater	mostly salt water
FOURTH TOOTH	inside mouth	outside mouth
HEAD SHAPE	U-shaped	V-shaped
COLOR	darker green	lighter tans and green
SENSORY PITS	only on jaw	all over body
ATTITUDE	less **aggressive** than crocodiles	more aggressive than alligators

19

Be Careful!

Whether it's a crocodile or an alligator you've spotted, make sure you don't get close. No matter what animal is in the water, it may mistake you for prey. Crocodiles are usually more aggressive than alligators, but they both can be very dangerous!

GLOSSARY

aggressive: showing readiness to attack

crush: to squeeze together to break something

pressure: a force that pushes on something else

prey: an animal that is hunted by other animals for food

reptile: an animal covered with scales or plates that breathes air, has a backbone, and lays eggs, such as a turtle, snake, lizard, or crocodile

snout: an animal's nose and mouth

swamp: an area with trees that is covered with water at least part of the time

FOR MORE INFORMATION

BOOKS

Beaver, Simon. *Crocs & Gators*. New York, NY: Cambridge University Press, 2013.

Marsico, Katie. *Saltwater Crocodiles*. New York, NY: Children's Press, 2014.

WEBSITES

American Alligator
animals.nationalgeographic.com/animals/reptiles/american-alligator/
Find out more about the American alligator at the National Geographic website.

Crocodile & Alligator Differences
sciencekids.co.nz/sciencefacts/animals/crocodilealligatordifferences.html
Find out how you can tell the difference between alligators and crocodiles in the wild.

INDEX